THE OFFICIAL  PET G

Care for you

Guinea Pig

Tina Hearne

Contents

Acknowledgements
Animal Graphics/Solitaire, Anne Cumbers Dr David Guiterman,
Spectrum Colour Library Ltd, Sue Streeter, Sally Anne Thompson, ZEFA
Illustrations by Terry Riley and Mike Woodhatch/David Lewis Artists

First published 1981
Second reprint 1983
Revised edition 1985
9 8 7 6 5 4

Published by William Collins Sons and Company Limited
London · Glasgow · Sydney · Auckland · Toronto · Johannesburg
© Royal Society for the Prevention of Cruelty to Animals 1981
Printed in Italy by New Interlitho, Milan

ISBN 0 00 410220 7

Collins

Record Card

Record sheet for your own guinea pig

photograph or portrait

Name

Toffee ~~Toffeendy~~

Date of birth
(actual or estimated)

Variety   **Sex**

Bolivian.   Male

Colour/description

brown with speck on forehead

Feeding notes   **Medical record**   **Breeding record**

abcess when

fust had him

Veterinary surgeon's name   **Surgery hours**

Practice address   **Tel. no.**

Choosing a Guinea Pig

The guinea pig, or cavy, is one of the most popular of the pet rodents. It is a grassland animal by nature and is quite easy to care for when the right facilities are available. The short-haired breeds need little more than warm, dry accommodation, a good herbivorous diet, and regular access to a grazing and exercise area.

Prospective owners should note that guinea pigs are not hardy enough to endure draughts, damp, and very cold weather, and in cool climates will need to be housed under shelter in the winter. A draughty lean-to roof over the hutch will not be adequate, but a well-built shed or outbuilding will be suitable if it is warmed, when necessary, with a small heater such as those used for greenhouses and garages.

For breeding purposes one male is usually kept with several females, but pet guinea pigs need the companionship of others, and it is recommended that two or more females be kept together. Adult males will not share accommodation without fighting.

Guinea pigs are docile with people, and soon become tame and tractable. They do not climb much and are not as agile as some of the smaller rodents. Their size and shape allow them to be easily handled by children.

A wide variety of breeds is available; however, the long-haired types need frequent grooming and are consequently the least suitable as pets.

As with most animals it is best to buy guinea pigs from their place of birth, and preferably from a professional breeder, rather than from any other source.

Children are able to lift guinea pigs with confidence. Their average weight is about 900g/2lb., and they seldom bite or struggle when handled.

The routine care of short-haired breeds is simple, but they should be kept under shelter in cold weather.

Varieties

Short-haired breeds
The so-called English or Bolivian breeds are the easiest of all to groom, retaining the short, smooth coat of the wild cavies.

Single-coloured specimens are known as Selfs, and each colour is recognized as a separate breed: Self White, Self Black, Self Cream, Self Beige, Self Golden, Self Lilac, Self Red, and Self Chocolate.

Other short-haired breeds have two or more colours, and often distinct body markings. Of these the Dutch is often seen, although those sold as pets are unlikely to have perfect markings. Breeders try to achieve an unbroken saddle band and a flash down the centre of the face in the basic white fur, separating the three dark areas – each side of the face and the hindquarters.

Agouti guinea pigs are said to resemble the wild cavies more than other breeds. They have a pepper and salt effect that is the result of the hairs being tipped with black. There are Gold, Silver, Salmon, Lemon and Cinnamon Agoutis.

Tortoiseshell and **Tortoiseshell and White** are other favourite breeds. The coats are patterned with blocks of black and red (tortoiseshell), or black, red and white (tortoiseshell and white), of roughly equal size, arranged alternately on either side of the body.

Himalayan guinea pigs are marked like Siamese cats, although the young do not show the coloured points at birth. The points – ears, nose, and feet – become defined when the young guinea pig is five or six months old.

Rough-haired breed
During the long period of domestication certain mutations of coat-type have occurred, and the rough-haired, or **Abyssinian**, is a particularly attractive example.

The hair of an Abyssinian is straight and coarse, and

Smooth-haired: Self Black

Long-haired: Peruvian

stands up to a height of 3cm/1½in all over the body, arranged in a pattern of rosettes, with a ridge along the spine. A show specimen would have ten rosettes: four around the saddle; two on each flank; and one on each shoulder.

Pet Abyssinians may show far less perfect markings, and many are the result of crossbreeding with smooth-haired guinea pigs. Such crossbreds may show only a single rosette.

The Abyssinians occur in a range of self colours, and also in the marked colours, for instance, Agouti and Tortoiseshell.

Long-haired breeds

The **Peruvian**, whose long, silky hair may well grow to floor length, or even longer in show specimens, is the best-known of the long-haired breeds. Fanciers frequently keep Peruvians with their long hair rolled up between shows. The hair falls towards the floor from a parting along the back, and covers the face. Obviously this is a variety for the show bench rather than for the garden enclosure.

More recent long-haired breeds are the **Sheltie**, similar to the Peruvian, but with hair growing back off the face in a long mane, and the **Coronet**, which looks just like the Sheltie, but with a crest or rosette on the head.

Rough-haired: Tortie/White

Roan Abyssinian

Golden Agouti

Tortoiseshell and White

Biology

Cavia porcellus is the scientific name, meaning the 'pig-like cavy'. Although rough and long-haired varieties may not appear to be very porcine, the smooth breeds, which are most like the wild cavies, rather resemble pigs in outline. The wide neck, the long body, and the rounded hindquarters without a tail are particularly pig-like, and if you add a curly tail and redraw the Roman nose as a snout, the likeness becomes clearer.

There is also a similarity of movement: sometimes, like pigs, these cavies 'trot', with the body lifted well clear of the ground, and moving more slowly than in their normal low, scurrying run.

Teeth The cheek teeth as well as the front incisor teeth grow continuously, and have to be worn down by constant wear. In contrast to rabbits, which use a side-to-side movement when chewing, guinea pigs grind food from front to back, and hay, raw vegetables and hard fruit all help to keep the teeth in trim. In addition, guinea pigs need a gnawing block. A freshly cut log with the bark left on is best, but avoid those from poisonous trees such as yew and laburnum.

At birth guinea pigs have their full set of teeth. Any difficulty with feeding may point to some abnormality in their dentition, generally overgrowth of the incisors, needing professional trimming.

Guinea pig or cavy? The use of the word cavy when referring to these animals is scientifically correct, and is favoured by the fanciers who run Cavy Clubs throughout the country. The general public, however, still clings to the more popular guinea pig, and either is acceptable.

The use of the word 'guinea', however, is curious, and has not been satisfactorily explained. There are several possibilities, and the most acceptable suggests that it is a corruption of Guiana. Originally guinea pigs were exported from the (then) Guiana coast of South America, from which the animals were first brought to Europe by Spanish sailors.

Social animals In their native grasslands, guinea pigs live as social animals, in family colonies. When kept as pets they should be housed together, if at all possible, in small compatible groups. Those deprived of the company of other guinea pigs will suffer from an unnatural isolation, and in particular circumstances the loss can even be physically harmful. A case in point is the problem of exposure. It sometimes happens, in Britain, that an unexpected cold snap will take owners unawares, and guinea pigs will be found suffering from exposure, having been left in an unprotected hutch, perhaps with too small a quantity of bedding. In such circumstances, several guinea pigs would huddle together for warmth, and perhaps survive quite well; in very similar circumstances, a lone guinea pig could well succumb.

Voice Guinea pigs have a whole range of vocal noises, of which the most often heard is an insistent 'wee-wee-wee' sound. Others include grunts, squeaks, chatterings, and chirrupings, so that at different times one may imagine they sound like a variety of other mammals, and quite often like birds.

Claws In the wild the claws are worn down continually as the guinea pigs constantly move across rough ground in order to graze. In captivity the four claws of each forefoot and the three of each hindfoot need to be worn down naturally, if possible, by exercising and grazing on the ground. When conditions are too soft to provide enough friction, or when the animals are kept for long periods on soft floor litter, or on deep straw, the claws may become overgrown. They may be trimmed slightly with animal nail clippers, taking care not to cut too near to the blood and nerve supply at the base of the nail. If in doubt about how far to cut, seek knowledgeable guidance.

Rodents The guinea pigs belong to the order of rodents, the gnawing animals, which must constantly wear down their continuously growing teeth or face starvation. This may happen because the jaws can no longer close, or perhaps because one unopposed incisor tooth grows until it locks into its opposite jaw, and so clamps both together (see Teeth).

The rodents themselves, which comprise the largest and most widespread order of mammals on earth, are divided into three sub-orders: Sciuromorpha (squirrels and beavers); Myomorpha (mice, rats, and hamsters); and Hystricomorpha (cavies, coypu, porcupines, and chinchilla).

The hystricomorphs are all native to the one geographical area of South America, Central America, and the Caribbean Islands, and it is to this sub-order that the guinea pigs, and all the cavies belong.

They have characteristically very long pregnancies, and consequently precocious young born with fur, teeth and open eyes. They are able to withstand surface life from the first day.

Many hystricomorphs have pregnancies of one hundred days or more. Guinea pigs have a pregnancy period of about 63 days, which is comparable to that of cats and dogs, and is much longer than the average gestation periods of the other major pet rodents: rabbit (31 days), gerbil (24 days), rat (22 days), mouse (21 days), Golden hamster (16 days).

Lack of tail An animal's tail may have many useful functions: to act as a support, balance, and rudder; to be a muffler, or fly swat; to store fat for the winter; even, among prehensile animals, to serve as another limb. When an animal like the guinea pig has no tail we have to accept that it serves no biological purpose and the appendage is lost through the long process of evolution.

Internally guinea pigs retain a line of minute tail vertebrae, but externally all that shows is a slight, round depression.

Guinea Pigs in South America

Cavies are indigenous to South America, where several different species are still to be found.

The wild ancestor of the domesticated guinea pig, *Cavia porcellus*, is thought to be the restless cavy, *Cavia cutleri*. This particular cavy is native to Peru, where it is a grazing animal, almost entirely dependent on grass for both food and shelter.

The restless cavies live in extended family groups in surface runs trodden through long grass, and protected above by the overhanging stems. The cavies may use rock crevices, or the abandoned burrows of other animals, but as far as is known they do not excavate for themselves.

Before the Spanish conquest of South America in the sixteenth century the now extinct Incas kept these animals for food, and even today the Peruvians breed them for the table, rather as certain breeds of rabbit are sometimes kept for their meat in Britain. Sailors were probably the first to keep cavies exclusively as pets, and introduce them to Europe from South America.

The grasslands of the lower slopes of the Andes are the natural habitat of the restless cavies of Peru from which the familiar pet guinea pigs are thought to be derived.

The Hutch Enclosure

Guinea pigs need a sturdy hutch, similar in design to that used for rabbits. Some hutches, which are rather too cramped for any but the smallest rabbit breeds, provide good accommodation for guinea pigs.

Two communicating compartments are recommended. One should have a wiremesh front, admitting enough light to make the compartment suitable for daytime use and, in particular, for feeding. The other needs a solid front so that it provides a dark, sheltered retreat for daytime rest periods and for night use. If the fronts are made as two hinged doors, then there is easy access to every part of the interior and cleaning is made simple (p 20).

The hutch must be raised off the ground, well clear of rising damp, and must be weatherproof.

The inside of the hutch needs to have containers for food and water, a rack for hay, a layer of peatmoss or other suitable floor litter, together with a generous quantity of hay or oat straw for the bedding compartment. If there is a roof overhang at the front of the hutch, the interior will be far better protected in wet weather.

During most of the year the hutch may be stood in an enclosure so that, in the daytime, the guinea pigs' accommodation can be extended by the use of a ramp.

Rocky caves, a log placed over a scrape of earth, drainpipes, piles of hay, and the hutch itself provide the cover these animals are so quick to seek. If there is any danger of attack from cats or dogs, then a cover of wiremesh stretched on a wooden frame must be used over the entire enclosure.

In very cold weather the guinea pigs will be at risk if left in an exposed hutch even if provided with plenty of bedding straw. As temperatures begin to fall, the hutch must be moved into the house, or into the shelter of a good shed or outbuilding.

A roomy enclosure with access to shelter allows guinea pigs freedom with maximum security. A mesh cover may be needed for protection from dogs and cats, and to keep sparrows from taking all the grain. At night the ramp should be removed and the guinea pigs shut up in the hutch which must be fitted with good safety catches or bolts.

The Grazing Ark

Guinea pigs kept in a hutch, without an enclosure, need a portable ark for both grazing and exercise. Those which have a permanent enclosure (p 10–11) benefit by having an ark in which they can feed naturally outside during part of the day. The grass in a hutch enclosure is soon worn down, and has very little chance to recover. By using an ark that is frequently moved onto fresh grass, guinea pigs are able to satisfy their very basic need to graze.

Soreness could be caused by wire netting used as a floor, and so an ark is better without one if it is to be used exclusively for guinea pigs, which make no attempt to escape by burrowing. If the base frame is well-made, and sturdy enough to rest squarely on the ground, then there is no danger that the guinea pigs will be able to crawl out from underneath.

An ark is for temporary use, and not a substitute for a hutch, so it is vital to provide a sheltered area, with hay for cover, which may be used as a retreat from any disturbance, or from rain and cold.

Indoor Exercising

An indoor play pen is ideal for those days when the weather is too wet, or too harsh, for guinea pigs to graze and exercise in the open air.

They have the same active quality that gives their ancestral species its name – the restless cavy – and they like to trot around their territory from time to time. They should not be shut in a hutch for long periods, but given opportunity to exercise even when the grazing area cannot be used.

Many owners are prepared to allow their guinea pigs some freedom in the house, but they tend to gnaw electric cables and the like, and may be safer in a play pen.

An indoor play pen is suitable for exercising guinea pigs in cold or damp weather when they would be at risk or uncomfortable outside.

The most convenient design, as in the illustration, is a large, shallow-sided tray that can be cleaned out easily with a dustpan and brush. If the play pen is mounted on runners or casters, it can be easily pushed aside when the room has to be cleaned.

The interior of the play pen must be made comfortable for the guinea pigs. They will need a shelter, preferably filled with loose-packed hay or straw that they can burrow into, a water bottle, food dishes, and a log for gnawing.

Newspapers spread on the base of the tray will make a highly absorbent layer, but should be spread with a good floor litter such as peatmoss or wood shavings.

Rough-haired Tortoiseshell and White with young

Peruvian

Peruvian

Bolivian

Feeding

Guinea pigs are by nature grazing animals and in the wild they live on the leaves, stems, and seeds of grasses and their associated plants. In captivity grass, hay, fresh vegetable matter and grain are all essential foodstuffs.

The use of an ark (pp 12–13) allows guinea pigs to graze safely each day, and is portable enough to be moved frequently to fresh areas of grass. If grass clippings are used they must be fed very fresh rather than left to ferment, and used only if quite free from chemicals.

Plenty of top quality hay is invaluable to these animals, and should be offered in a hay rack to prevent it being trodden and soiled underfoot.

Provided that they have not been contaminated by chemicals, lots of wild plants may also be fed, including such favourites as groundsel, dandelion, clover, vetch, shepherd's purse, chickweed, sow thistle, and cow parsley. Because some wild plants are poisonous, care must be taken not to offer any except those known to be safe.

Raw fruit and vegetables help to satisfy the guinea pigs' particular need for a regular vitamin C intake.

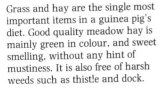

Grass and hay are the single most important items in a guinea pig's diet. Good quality meadow hay is mainly green in colour, and sweet smelling, without any hint of mustiness. It is also free of harsh weeds such as thistle and dock.

Guinea pigs do not use their forelimbs as hands, and so they feed better if the vegetables are cut into chunks.

Besides grass, hay, wild plants, and raw vegetables and fruit, guinea pigs also need some cereal food each day: crushed oats, proprietary grain mixture sold for guinea pigs, wholemeal bread, and possibly bran. This cereal compensates for the seeding grasses they would eat in the wild, and should be fed twice a day, either dry, or as a crumbly mash made with hot or cold milk or water. Remove mash bowls after feeding times to avoid left-over food going sour. Bran should not be fed dry, but in a mash.

Because feeding is a major activity of guinea pigs, fresh food needs to be available at all times, including night, when they need hay and vegetables.

The amount of water taken varies, particularly according to how much fresh food is available, but must always be within the guinea pigs' reach. Drip feed bottles need scouring to prevent the build-up of algae.

Useful food supplements include a mineral lick, cod liver oil in winter, and possibly vitamin C.

Groundsel and dandelion are two of the most popular of the many wild plants which may safely be fed to guinea pigs. Some plants, however, are poisonous, including bindweeds, foxglove, yew, buttercups, bryony, nightshades, privet, travellers' joy, dog's mercury, ragworts, wood anemone, wild arum, sorrels, docks, poppies and laburnum.

Hygiene

Hygiene It is said that one advantage of keeping guinea pigs, rather than some of the other rodent pets, is that they are odourless. This is true, but even so there will be an unpleasant smell if they are kept in a hutch that is not cleaned out for days on end. Flooring or floor litter saturated with urine, piles of faeces – even those deposited neatly in one corner, as many owners find – and decaying vegetables will soon make the hutch unhygienic.

It should be understood that a guinea pig's hutch in constant use must be cleaned out daily. This routine attention includes removing droppings, checking the floor litter is dry, and replacing that in the damp corner if necessary. One should tidy the sleeping compartment, and make sure the amount of bedding is adequate for the weather conditions. Replenishing hay and other feedstuffs, and washing and refilling the drip feed bottle are other daily tasks. Periodically a hutch will need to be thoroughly cleaned and scrubbed, and allowed to dry completely before being used again.

The important daily task of hutch cleaning is made much easier if the hutch is properly designed (pp 10–11), and if cleaning tools, hay, bedding straw, floor litter and so on are kept in an orderly fashion and conveniently close.

When the animals spend most of their time outside in an enclosure or, if safety allows, free in the garden, then cleaning the hutch every other day may suffice. Even so, food, water, and bedding must be checked daily.

Grooming It is very important that rough-haired and long-haired varieties should be kept in good, sanitary conditions, or their hair is liable to become matted together in a most unpleasant way. Abyssinian, Peruvian, Sheltie, and Crested Sheltie varieties, together with rough or long-haired crossbreds, ought to be groomed daily. Brush the way the fur grows, using a stiff brush that will remove loose hairs, tangles, and pieces of twig, dry leaves or burrs that may have become enmeshed. Gentle but firm insistence on daily grooming from a young age for all these breeds will gradually accustom them to it as a matter of routine. It will help keep them tame, and also afford the owner opportunity to observe their condition carefully, and take action if need be (p 26).

Grooming is another job for owners of rough and long-haired breeds of guinea pig. Their long hair can quickly become soiled and matted unless they are kept in very clean living conditions, and groomed daily.

Handling and Sexing

Guinea pigs are quite the easiest of the pet rodents to handle, many being readily tamed and generally docile. They are unlikely to struggle or bite when picked up competently by their regular handler, but even so great care should be taken not to drop them. Because they are rather heavy for their size, and not as agile as other rodents, they are vulnerable to injury of the limbs or spine if dropped, even from a small height, or if they are subjected to rough handling.

The recommended way to lift a guinea pig is, as in the illustration, with two hands – one around the hind quarters, to support the animal's weight, the other around the shoulders, to control the movement of the forelimbs.

It is important that, particularly towards the end of her pregnancy, a gravid sow should be handled with great care and gentleness, and then only when necessary. There is some danger that the young could be still-born as a result of rough or excessive handling while they were in

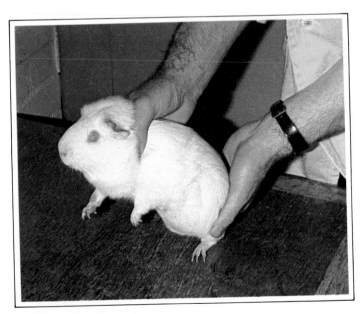

Correct handling. One hand supporting the weight of the hind quarters; the other supporting the shoulders.

the womb. By the age of eight to ten weeks, young guinea pigs will become sexually mature and need segregating to avoid unwanted pregnancies. They may be sexed at this age if cradled in the crook of the handler's arm so that the genital opening is accessible. Gentle pressure around the opening will show up the Y-shaped slit of the female, and will extrude the penis of the male. The presence of nipples is no indication of sex in guinea pigs. Both males and females have two, positioned low down on the abdomen.

The males may be expected to be larger than the females right from birth. By the time they are adult a boar may measure perhaps 25cm/10in in length and weigh 1000g/35oz; a sow perhaps 20cm/8in and 850g/30oz.

In temperament the males are more assertive than the females, and likely to fight among each other, although not all females are docile. Some highly strung individuals may be too aggressive to live with other females, and any female may turn on a male if unwilling to be mated.

Genital openings of guinea pig:
Left   Male, showing extruded penis
Right   Female, showing Y-shaped slit

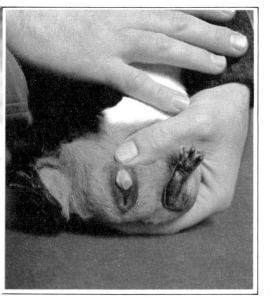
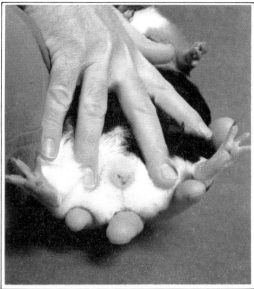

Ailments

Respiratory infections Symptoms similar to those associated with the common cold in man are made worse by poor living conditions, and can develop into pneumonia. Rehousing the guinea pigs in isolation in a dry, warm, and roomy cage will often bring about an improvement and stop the spread of these respiratory infections. If in doubt, or if the symptoms persist, seek veterinary advice.

Loss of balance A guinea pig which holds its head to one side and which may veer round in circles, quite unable to walk in a straight line, is showing symptoms of middle ear disease and professional advice should be sought.

Pseudotuberculosis Enlarged glands in the neck and growths in the abdomen may be caused by a serious condition known as pseudotuberculosis. Sometimes death is rapid, but other variations of the condition may cause a slow deterioration in the guinea pig over several weeks. This is a highly infectious disease and veterinary advice must be sought.

Salmonellosis An organism of the salmonella group causes rapid loss of condition followed by collapse. This very serious disease has a high mortality rate and spreads quickly through large breeding or laboratory colonies. Veterinary attention is vital because the most rigorous cleaning and disinfecting is necessary before it is safe to introduce new stock into the accommodation after an outbreak. Animals that do survive an attack may act as carriers and cause subsequent outbreaks. There is also a hazard to human health, and therefore particular care over personal hygiene must be taken.

Diarrhoea Diarrhoea may be due to an intestinal infection, introduced by way of contaminated or frosted vegetable matter, or due to a sudden change in diet. It may also be a non-specific symptom of disease and, if it persists, or occurs with other symptoms, advice should be sought.

Constipation This may be due to disease, lack of roughage, or too dry a diet (perhaps with too much cereal and pellet food), fed without sufficient water.

Vitamin C deficiency Guinea pigs, and especially pregnant sows, have a particular need for a high daily vitamin C intake. A deficiency may lead to scurvy, and a loss of resistance to other diseases, although no such risk occurs if the diet is high in fresh, raw fruit and vegetable, grass and suitable wild plants. Guinea pigs not feeding adequately because of overgrown teeth (p 6) may not take in enough of the vitamin, even though the right foods are available to them. Pellets fed without fresh vegetable matter, or those prepared for other animals, may not contain enough vitamin C to meet this need.

Stripping hair This abnormal behaviour, when guinea pigs strip their own hair as far as they can reach or strip each other, tends to occur in the long-haired breeds. Some young are made quite hairless in this way by their own parents. The cause may be boredom and, in particular, the lack of something for these grazing animals to chew. This is one reason why it is essential to give guinea pigs as much hay as they will eat, and to keep them in pairs or small groups in as interesting an environment as possible.

Wounds Torn ears, sore hocks, and skin abrasion may be the result of keeping incompatible guinea pigs together. Consult a veterinary surgeon if the wound is serious, or becomes infected, but otherwise bathe in a mild antiseptic solution. Keep males apart, and separate females if they constantly fight and kick. Normally compatible guinea pigs may fight when overcrowded.

Parasites Guinea pigs are usually free of parasites unless there are infected cats and dogs, for instance, in the house. They may, however, become infested with lice, perhaps from infected hay or straw. Either bath the guinea pig with a medicated shampoo or treat with a mild insecticide powder. Repeat the treatment once a week, and if in any doubt or difficulty, seek veterinary help.

Overgrown teeth and claws In common with all the captive rodents, guinea pigs may sometimes be unable to wear down their teeth or trim their claws naturally.

The Healthy Guinea Pig

Guinea pigs should live to between four and seven years or even longer, if they are bred from strong stock and are well-cared for in clean, spacious accommodation with protection from cold and damp, suitable food, plenty of exercise and somewhere to hide.

When they do fall ill prompt veterinary attention is needed because, like so many small animals, guinea pigs deteriorate quickly, and have rather poor powers of recuperation.

Some of the external signs of health are listed.

Anus	clean, no staining or scouring
Appetite	good, eating frequently and during night
Breathing	silent and regular
Body	firm and well-fleshed, no growths or swellings
Claws	short and trim, no splits
Coat	clean, no soiling by faeces or urine; no tangles, skin eruptions, or parasites
Demeanour	alert, responsive and inquisitive, posture normal, not flattened
Droppings	small, elongated pellets about 1cm/½in long
Ears	rose petal shaped, turning downwards, not torn, no discharge
Eyes	wide open and bright, no cloudiness or discharge
Feet	strong and well-formed, no soreness of hocks, weight distributed evenly
Mouth	clean, with no slobbering
Movement	rapid shuffling, close to the ground, and a 'trot' with body held high off the ground, freezes when alarmed
Nose	clear of any discharge or dried mucus
Teeth	worn down naturally on hard food and gnawing blocks

Life History

Scientific name	*Cavia porcellus*
Gestation period	63 days (approx.)
Litter size	2–4 average
Birth weight	85–90g/about 3oz (average)
Eyes open	at birth
Weaning age	21–28 days
Weaning weight	about 250g/8½oz
Puberty	males 8–10 weeks females 4–5 weeks
Adult weight	males 1000g/35oz females 850g/30oz
Best age to breed	12 weeks (see p 28)
Oestrus (or season)	every two weeks (approx.)
Duration of oestrus	15 hours (approx.)
Retire from breeding	2 years (see p 28)
Life expectancy	4–7 years

Reproduction

As a general rule it is inadvisable to breed from young females of any species who may have reached puberty, but who are too immature in behaviour to deal with their own young patiently and competently. The same applies if they are too physically immature for the pelvis to have reached an adequate size to prevent pain and difficulty (dystocia) during the birth process.

The case of the guinea pig is rather different. There may be a greater risk of dystocia if the guinea pig does not have her first litter while she is still young. Once fully grown, the pelvic bones fuse, leaving her with a rigid, perhaps undersized pelvis, and this may cause difficult births and a shorter breeding span than normal.

Pet keepers who want to breed should be aware that there is an alternative school of thought that says guinea pigs should not breed before they are six months old.

For this reason it is recommended that guinea pigs should be first mated at the relatively young age of 12 weeks. The litter will then be born before the mother reaches full maturity, and before the two halves of the pelvis fuse firmly together. Subsequent births should be trouble-free. Many females first mated when very young breed successfully and easily beyond the age of 18–24 months, which is usually quoted as the time to retire guinea pigs from breeding. Even so, it is advisable, as always, to retire the older stock from breeding to make way for younger and more vigorous animals to continue a healthy line.

If the boar is left with the sow permanently, it is possible for her to bear five litters a year. Such an intensive rate of breeding is most undesirable among pet guinea pigs, not least because it will produce far more young than could be homed satisfactorily. It is better if the boar and sow are separated for periods, to avoid the chances of pregnancy. In particular, many owners find it advisable to house a pregnant sow alone for a week or two before her litter is due, because she needs very careful handling and quiet conditions then, and leave her alone to bring up her family until weaning age. If the boar were left with the sow she would be likely to become pregnant again immediately after giving birth.

Those who do want to breed from their guinea pigs are urged to join a good Cavy Club, for experienced help, advice and tuition before starting.

Pregnant females drink thirstily and will take milk as well as water. Their diet must be increased to support the unborn or suckling young, and if there are more than three in the litter they will need extra milk since she has only two mammary glands.

It has already been said that guinea pigs are intolerant of low temperatures; similarly they are liable to suffer heat exhaustion during spells of very hot weather, or if they are kept in poorly ventilated conditions. A heavily pregnant sow is particularly vulnerable in this respect. If she is kept in a hutch it must be moved to a shady position and hosed with cold water.

The Young

The delightful young of the guinea pig are born with a full coat, with their eyes open, their teeth already cut, able to move around – supporting their weight on the legs – and attempting to take solid food within a day or two.

This exceptional maturity at birth makes them the loveliest of all the usual pet rodent babies. They are born after a long gestation of about 63 days (p 7), usually in rather small litters, and single births are not uncommon. Average birth weight for the females is 85g/3oz; 90g/$3\frac{1}{2}$oz for the males. Single birth weights may be as much as 150g/$5\frac{1}{4}$oz.

Because they are so well-developed, there is very little likelihood of new-born cavies being at risk from their parents, as is the case with mice, rats, rabbits, and gerbils.

Suckling continues for about 3 weeks, but the young are best left with the sow until the age of 4 or 5 weeks when they weigh perhaps 250g/$8\frac{1}{2}$oz. There is no danger in leaving both sow and boar with the young to live as a small colony, although of course there is the risk of the sow becoming pregnant again.

The young are not able to mate each other before the males reach puberty at 8–10 weeks, although in a family group the females would be at risk of being mated by the boar once they reached puberty at perhaps 4–5 weeks.

These are social animals, and if they are rehomed at the age of 8 weeks, it is very unfair to expect them to live a solitary life in captivity. For this reason the females are most often recommended as pets, since they will usually live peaceably in small groups of two or more.

Guinea pigs have an enduring reputation as one of the most successful pet animals and for their agreeable natures. The long-haired breeds need some extra attention, by way of daily grooming, but all are fairly simple to care for if their accommodation has been well thought out in advance, and proves adequate in severe weather, and if the very necessary chore of frequent cleaning out is not too daunting a task.

Female with new born young

Index